Original title:
In the Glow of Dreams

Copyright © 2024 Creative Arts Management OÜ
All rights reserved.

Author: Robert Ashford
ISBN HARDBACK: 978-9916-90-664-4
ISBN PAPERBACK: 978-9916-90-665-1

Ethereal Echoes

Whispers dance on twilight's breeze,
Carried forth by ancient trees.
Shadows blend with fading light,
Echoes shimmer, taking flight.

Through the mist, a vision glows,
In silence deep, where magic flows.
Stars unite in cosmic grace,
Ethereal dreams we now embrace.

Horizons of Light

Beneath the sky, we see it rise,
A spectrum born from violet skies.
Golden rays ignite the morn,
New beginnings, brightly worn.

Waves of color, pure delight,
Chasing shadows, holding tight.
Every dawn, a canvas bright,
Horizons painted, full of light.

The Fires of Inspiration

In quiet corners, embers glow,
Igniting thoughts from deep below.
Passion's flame, it flickers near,
Inspiration whispers clear.

With every spark, a story spins,
A dance of dreams where hope begins.
Through raging storms, the fire burns,
The heart ignites, the spirit turns.

Glimpses of the Infinite

Stars align in cosmic weave,
Each one holds a tale to believe.
In the void, a light reflects,
Glimpses sent, the mind connects.

Across the realms of space and time,
A tapestry, a whispered rhyme.
Endless journeys, we partake,
Infinite wonders, no mistake.

Echoes of Starlit Fantasies

In the quiet night sky, whispers roam,
Dreams woven in silver, far from home.
Stars blink in rhythm, secrets unfold,
Tales of adventures, waiting to be told.

Embers of light in a celestial sea,
Guiding lost spirits, setting them free.
With every heartbeat, wishes take flight,
Dancing through shadows, embracing the night.

Reflections of a Moonlit Heart

The moon casts a glow, soft and sincere,
Lighting the edges of paths we hold dear.
Water ripples gently, serenely it sways,
Mirroring moments in silvery rays.

Whispers of longing in silken embrace,
Hearts intertwine in the tenderest space.
Shadows may linger, but hope finds a way,
Guided by love, as night turns to day.

Dances Beneath the Stars

Underneath the cosmos, where dreams intertwine,
Feet brush the earth, hearts sync and align.
With laughter as music, we twirl and we sway,
As constellations bear witness to play.

Each step a moment, each twirl a delight,
Lost in the magic of the vast starry night.
Light bodies are weightless, freedom we feel,
In the embrace of the cosmos, our truths we reveal.

Ethereal Journeys

On wings of wonder, we soar through the skies,
Boundless horizons, where imagination lies.
Clouds paint the canvas of worlds yet unseen,
In the heart of the cosmos, we dance in between.

Voices of stardust, sing soft lullabies,
Guiding our hearts where the dreams never die.
With every new journey, we write our own tale,
Chasing the light, we shall never grow stale.

Celestial Nightfall

Stars awaken in the sky,
Whispers of the twilight sigh.
Moon's soft gaze upon the earth,
Veiling dreams in gentle mirth.

Clouds drift like secrets untold,
Cradling night in arms of gold.
Each flicker, a story starts,
Painting shadows on our hearts.

Shimmering Aspirations

In the morning, dew drops gleam,
Hope unfurls like a shining beam.
Dreams take flight on gentle wings,
Carving paths where freedom sings.

Every heartbeat, a wish made true,
In the garden where hopes renew.
Chasing visions, bold and bright,
Together we ignite the night.

The Light in the Shadows

In the corner where silence creeps,
A flicker of light in darkness leaps.
Hope resides in quiet spaces,
Filling voids with warm embraces.

Through the gloom, we find our way,
Guided by the light of day.
Whispers dance in shadows deep,
Promising dreams that never sleep.

Dreamweaver's Embrace

In the realm where wishes weave,
Gentle hands begin to cleave.
Every thread a tale untold,
Cradled in the arms of bold.

Stars align in vivid hues,
Painting skies with dreams we choose.
As the night wraps us in grace,
We are held in time and space.

Nebula of Silent Wishes

In a sky of velvet black,
Stars whisper secrets and dreams,
Shimmering softly, they beckon,
To the heart where hope gleams.

Across the cosmic expanse,
Silent wishes flow like streams,
Cascading through the void,
Glowing bright with endless beams.

Glimmers of what might be,
Dance in a fleeting night,
Cocooned in the fabric of time,
Painting futures with their light.

Beneath the starlit gaze,
We weave our silent desires,
In the nebula of longing,
Our spirits ignite like fires.

Canvas of Unspoken Hopes

In shadows where dreams linger,
A canvas waits with hues untold,
Brush strokes of unvoiced wishes,
Pastel futures, brave and bold.

Each color whispers soft stories,
Of the hearts that yearn and sigh,
Painting visions of tomorrow,
In the silence, they comply.

The artist with a gentle hand,
Fills the void with vibrant light,
As hopes bloom in secret gardens,
Glistening through the quiet night.

Behind the canvas of silence,
Lies a world waiting to unfold,
Unspoken hopes together dance,
In a gallery of pure gold.

Light Beneath the Distant Horizon

In the twilight of the day,
Where the sky kisses the sea,
There lies a light, ever fading,
A promise for you and me.

Horizon whispers softly,
Of journeys yet to begin,
Glimmers of hope on the water,
Where dreams and reality spin.

Chasing that distant glow,
We walk on paths of desire,
Every step towards the future,
Carrying hearts full of fire.

Beneath the vast expanse,
We find solace in the night,
For every dusk brings a dawn,
And love will always find its light.

Nighttime Chronicles of Dreams

Every night tells a story,
In the hush of starlit skies,
Chronicles of whispered wishes,
Where forgotten longing lies.

The moon, a gentle keeper,
Holds the secrets of the night,
While shadows dance on silence,
In a realm of silver light.

Dreamers gather in the dark,
Where imagination takes flight,
Sailing through the depths of sleep,
Chasing visions, bold and bright.

With each dawn, tales are woven,
From the threads of night's embrace,
In the nighttime chronicles,
We find dreams that time won't erase.

Fragments of a Shining Heart

In the shadows, a glimmer lies,
Hope and love within the sighs,
Pieces scattered, yet so bright,
Shining softly in the night.

Each fragment tells a story clear,
Of laughter lost and hidden fear,
Together woven, strong and true,
A heart reborn, a vibrant hue.

The Ember of Ambitions

Deep within the soul it glows,
A flicker where the passion flows,
With every challenge, flames ignite,
Pushing forward with all its might.

Though storms may rage and shadows loom,
This ember thrives, it dares to bloom,
Chasing dreams that dance like fire,
Fueling the heart's relentless desire.

Threads of Glistening Dreams

Silken strands of hope so fine,
Interwoven by design,
Whispers of the future gleam,
Woven tightly into a dream.

Each thread holds a promise bold,
A tapestry of stories told,
In every hue, in every gleam,
Together weaving life's grand theme.

Sparkling Whispers

In the silence, secrets fly,
Caught like stars in midnight sky,
Softly spoken, truths unmasked,
Bringing light, as shadows bask.

Every whisper bears a spark,
Igniting joy within the dark,
A glimmer, a sweet refrain,
Echoing love through joy and pain.

Where Night Meets Day

In twilight's embrace, shadows creep,
The sun bids farewell, the stars begin to leap.
A canvas of colors, dusk unfurls,
Dreams gently whisper, as night softly swirls.

The horizon glows, a soft golden hue,
With every heartbeat, the world feels anew.
Crickets sing softly, a lullaby sweet,
Where night meets day, the magic's complete.

The Light that Beckons

In the distance, a flicker ignites,
A beacon of hope, where darkness fights.
With every step forward, shadows retreat,
The light that beckons, a path to our feet.

Casting away doubts, it brightens the grey,
Guiding lost souls, come what may.
A warmth that surrounds, like a tender embrace,
The light that beckons, our fears it will chase.

Manifesting Reflections

In the mirror of dreams, visions collide,
Thoughts become whispers, with nowhere to hide.
Mirages of wishes, they dance in the mind,
Manifesting reflections, both tender and kind.

A tapestry woven with threads of desire,
Each glimpse a promise, feeding the fire.
In the silence of moments, truth takes its form,
Manifesting reflections, we weather the storm.

Garden of Shimmering Thoughts

Among petals and whispers, ideas bloom bright,
A garden of thoughts, where dreams take flight.
Sunshine and shadows, entwined as they play,
In this sanctuary, we find our way.

The fragrance of hope, like dew on the grass,
In this haven of wonders, let moments amass.
Each glimmer a spark, igniting our heart,
In the garden of thoughts, we all take part.

Chasing Ethereal Shadows

In the twilight's gentle embrace,
Whispers dance, just out of grace.
Footsteps lost along the way,
Chasing dreams that fade to gray.

Moonlit paths weave tales untold,
In the night, the heart grows bold.
Fleeting shapes in silent flight,
Guide the seeker through the night.

Lighted Steps of the Soul

With every step, a story glows,
Illuminating where one goes.
In shadows cast by hopes held high,
The soul ignites beneath the sky.

Gentle beams of warmth and grace,
Lead the heart to a sacred place.
Each light a memory, softly spun,
Together, we shine, forever one.

The Starry Tapestry

Stars ignite in cosmic flight,
Woven threads of endless night.
Each spark a dream, a wish unfurled,
A tapestry of a boundless world.

Constellations whisper low,
Guiding souls where they must go.
In this vault, our stories blend,
A celestial dance that has no end.

Flickering Hopes

In the dark, a candle's glow,
Flickering brightly, soft and slow.
Each flame a wish, a hidden plea,
A beacon of what's yet to be.

Through the storm, they dance and sway,
Reminding hearts to find their way.
With every flicker, dreams revive,
In the dark, our hopes survive.

The Heart's Little Secrets

In whispers soft, the heart does keep,
A treasure trove, emotions deep.
Flickers bright, a silent fire,
Yearning dreams, and quiet desire.

Like shadows dance, in twilight's light,
Unraveled tales, hidden from sight.
A gentle sigh, a fleeting glance,
In these moments, we find our chance.

Though words may fail, the heart can speak,
In tangled paths, it's brave, yet weak.
With every beat, it holds the key,
To all the truths that long to be.

So cherish well, the secrets held,
In chambers where our love has dwelled.
For in the silence, bonds we find,
The heart's true language, intertwined.

Lighthouses of the Mind

In stormy seas, they guide the way,
With steadfast beams, through night and day.
A beacon bright, on cliffs they stand,
Offering hope, a guiding hand.

In shadows deep, our thoughts can drift,
Yet lighthouses shine, a precious gift.
Through fog and doubt, they help us see,
The path ahead, where we should be.

With every wave, we learn and grow,
In currents fierce, the tides may flow.
But lighthouses hold, and never sway,
Their light remains, come what may.

So in our minds, let wisdom bloom,
Like lighthouses bright, dispel the gloom.
For in the chaos, calm we'll find,
The guiding light, of our own mind.

Mosaics of Light

In fragments bright, the colors blend,
Creating art, where shadows end.
Each piece unique, a story told,
In vibrant hues, the truth unfolds.

With every shard, a memory shines,
A fleeting glance, where heart aligns.
Together stitched, in patterns grand,
A tapestry, by fate's own hand.

In crooked paths, we search for grace,
In broken tiles, we find our place.
For life is rich, with all its flaws,
A mosaic bright, the heart's own cause.

So hold each piece, in gentle light,
For every moment, wrong or right.
Together weave, in love's own might,
The beautiful dance, of life's delight.

Stars in Our Eyes

In the velvet sky we gaze,
Twinkling orbs ignite our phase.
Whispers of dreams, daringly stray,
Guided by starlight, we find our way.

Hearts beat soft under the glow,
Constellations dance, a gentle flow.
Each spark a wish, a promise anew,
Holding our hopes in the night's hue.

The cosmos breaths a tender song,
In this moment, we each belong.
With every heartbeat, the universe sighs,
Together, we're woven with stars in our eyes.

Celestial Caress

Moonlight spills like silken threads,
Wrapping dreams in softest beds.
Gentle breezes carry the night,
In their embrace, all feels right.

Stars wink and giggle, so carefree,
Painting secrets none can see.
While shadows linger, warm and light,
The world sleeps under velvet night.

A cosmic dance of fate and grace,
Lost in the universe's embrace.
With every twinkle, I feel the bless,
Of the night's sweet, celestial caress.

When Night Breathes Bright

When night unfurls her silken shawl,
Stars awaken, answering the call.
Each glimmer a tale from afar,
As dreams take flight like a shooting star.

The moon, a lantern in the dark,
Guides the way with a golden spark.
In the hush, magic softly stirs,
Awakening wonders in her spurs.

In this symphony of night's delight,
Every shadow holds stories tight.
When silence whispers and time feels right,
We live in dreams when night breathes bright.

Secrets of the Dappled Dream

Softly whispered in twilight's gleam,
Lie the secrets of the dappled dream.
In the stillness, the heart will know,
Where the wildest imaginations flow.

Through the forest where shadows play,
Magic lingers in the softest sway.
Each leaf a keeper of silent lore,
Guarding the spirit of tales before.

In the cradle of night, stars take flight,
Painting the canvas, pure and bright.
Holding whispers of wishes made,
A tapestry of hope, never to fade.

Threads of Stardust and Wishes

In the night, whispers soar,
Dreams woven like threads of gold.
Each star holds a silent lore,
A tapestry of tales untold.

Wishes cast upon the breeze,
Glittering in the moon's soft glow.
Hearts dance like the rustling leaves,
In the magic of night's flow.

Grains of light fall from above,
Kissed by hope and starlit grace.
Threads of dreams, the heart will love,
In this vast, enchanting space.

Through the cosmos, spirits fly,
Embracing all that lies in sight.
The universe, vast and high,
Weaves our dreams with threads of light.

The Glow of Uncharted Realms

In shadows deep, a light breaks free,
Uncharted realms, where dreams ignite.
Mysteries unfold, like leaves of trees,
In the garden of the starry night.

Whispers of worlds that softly gleam,
Calling forth the restless heart's flight.
We wander through the woven dream,
Guided by the glow of twilight.

Veils of mist conceal the way,
Yet, hope illuminates the path.
In the quiet, where shadows play,
The glow reveals the aftermath.

Each star a beacon, bright and bold,
Leading us to where wishes bloom.
In the vastness, stories told,
Awake the night's enchanting gloom.

Starry-Eyed Musings

Gazing up at the endless sea,
Stars like diamonds in the dark.
Thoughts drift softly, wild and free,
Igniting dreams with each bright spark.

Whispers from the cosmic tides,
Paint the mind with tales of old.
On this canvas, imagination rides,
Through the journeys of the bold.

In the silence, the heart can hear,
Echoes of the past's embrace.
Starry-eyed, we shed our fear,
Finding magic in this place.

A moment lost in the expanse,
Where reflections of the soul align.
In each twinkle, a timeless dance,
Carving dreams in the stars' design.

Radiant Treasures of the Night

Beneath the veil of twilight's grace,
Treasures gleam with soft delight.
In their glow, a hidden place,
Offers peace within the night.

Moonbeams weave through the tall trees,
Painting dreams on whispered sighs.
Each shadow holds the gentle breeze,
Where the spirit freely flies.

Stars unfold their ancient tales,
Guiding hearts with radiant light.
In their warmth, the coldness pales,
As dreams take flight within the night.

Unseen wonders spark and glow,
Leading us to realms unknown.
Radiant treasures softly flow,
In the sphere where love has grown.

Secrets in the Twilight

Whispers linger in the night,
Shadows dance without a light.
Beneath the stars, dreams take flight,
Hidden truths in soft twilight.

Crickets sing a solemn tune,
Breezes carry scents of June.
In the darkness, secrets bloom,
Veiled in the gentle moon's loom.

Echoes fade and time stands still,
Hearts are bound by fate and will.
In this hour, the world is hushed,
Into the night, our souls are flushed.

Secrets linger, softly spun,
Tales of love, both lost and won.
In this moment, all we find,
Are the whispers of the mind.

The Illusion of Dawn

The night surrenders to the morn,
Colors blend where dreams are born.
In the stillness, shadows take flight,
Deceptive hues, a fleeting sight.

Birds awaken with a song,
Nature's chorus, pure and strong.
Yet beneath that rosy hue,
Lies the truth, both bold and blue.

Promises of light unfold,
Stories waiting to be told.
But in the glow of breaking day,
Fleeting moments drift away.

Awakening hearts feel the thrill,
Yet time moves on, it cannot stand still.
In the whisper of the dawn's embrace,
We find the dreams that time must chase.

Beneath the Velvet Veil

Silence drapes the evening sky,
Stars twinkle in a hushed sigh.
Wrapped in darkness, dreams reveal,
Mysteries lie beneath the veil.

A shroud of calm, the world asleep,
In the shadows, secrets keep.
Hidden whispers, tender, pale,
Lurking gently, beneath the veil.

Moonlight casts a silver beam,
Guiding lost souls in a dream.
In its glow, emotions sail,
As they wander, beneath the veil.

Timeless stories start to weave,
In this realm, we dare believe.
With hearts alight, we unveil,
The magic held beneath the veil.

Murmurs of the Celestial

Glistening eyes adorn the night,
Stars converse in radiant light.
Galaxies spin in cosmic play,
Murmurs echo, far away.

Silver beams, they stretch and weave,
Nature's tapestry, we perceive.
In the hush, the cosmos sighs,
Whispering secrets from the skies.

Each twinkle tells a story bright,
From distant worlds that spark delight.
In the silence, we may hear,
Murmurs soft, both far and near.

As we gaze with awe and fear,
In the stillness, truth draws near.
Let the stardust flow and glisten,
For in the dark, the heavens listen.

Tides of Bright Desires

Waves of longing crash on shores,
Each ebb and flow, the spirit soars.
With stars as guides, we chase the night,
Desires dance within the light.

Whispers of dreams in salty air,
A symphony of wishes rare.
The cosmos hums a gentle tune,
While hearts align beneath the moon.

In every tide, a story breathes,
Of what we seek and what heaves.
As currents shift, our hopes arise,
Each wave carries bright desires.

Ride the rhythm, feel the pull,
Moments fleeting, hearts so full.
In this embrace, the world conspired,
Our souls connected, dreams inspired.

Embracing the Unseen

In shadows deep where whispers dwell,
The heart finds peace in silent spell.
Through veils of night, hope starts to gleam,
A world awakened in the dream.

Unfolding layers, truth concealed,
Soft echoes speak, yet are revealed.
With every breath, the unseen sings,
A dance of light on fragile wings.

Beneath the surface, life abides,
In quiet waters, calm resides.
A journey sought beyond the sight,
In darkness blooms the hidden light.

Embrace the void, let fears release,
In stillness find a sweet release.
For in the unseen, love will tether,
An unseen world, forever together.

Luminescent Pathways

Beneath the stars, a road appears,
With every step, we shed our fears.
The glow of dusk ignites the way,
Guiding souls through night to day.

Each footprint glimmers on the ground,
With laughter's echo all around.
In twilight's hue, our spirits rise,
To dance as one beneath the skies.

A journey marked by love's embrace,
In woven light, we find our place.
Through winding paths, our hearts will soar,
Together we can seek for more.

So follow light where shadows play,
Through luminous nights, we'll find our way.
For in the glow of every chance,
We pave our dreams with cosmic dance.

The Secret Garden of Stars

In velvet night, a garden blooms,
Where secret hopes dispel the glooms.
With petals soft, and fragrance sweet,
The universe lies at our feet.

Whispers dance on night's cool breeze,
As cosmic tales weave through the trees.
Each star a story, bright and true,
In this haven, dreams renew.

A sanctuary of the heart,
Where light and shadow play their part.
In every glimmer, we will find,
The secrets held in love entwined.

So roam this realm, let wonder rise,
In the secret garden of the skies.
For in this space, where magic flows,
A world of dreams forever grows.

Breath of Celestial Ambitions

In the silent glow of dreams,
Stars weave tales of silent schemes.
Whispers dance on cosmic winds,
Guiding hearts where hope begins.

Adventures spark in dusky skies,
With every breath, the universe sighs.
Embers of light ignite the void,
In celestial realms, ambitions unfold.

Awake we rise, our spirits soar,
Chasing visions of distant shores.
With stardust dreams, we paint the night,
In the breath of hopes, we find our flight.

Together we carve the path untried,
With each heartbeat, our journey wide.
In the vastness, we find our place,
In celestial dreams, we embrace our grace.

Flickers of a Magical Slumber

Nestled deep in twilight's fold,
Where whispers of enchantment hold.
Flickers of dreams in gentle sway,
Guide the heart where shadows play.

Fairy lights and murmured sighs,
Bathe the world in soft goodbyes.
As moonbeams dance on pillow's hue,
The magic stirs, a night anew.

With each breath, the starlight glows,
Carrying tales only night knows.
In slumber's grip, we drift away,
To realms where fantasies gently lay.

Awake, we breathe the dreams we've spun,
In magic's glow, we become one.
Through flickers, we chase the lost,
In slumber's arms, we pay the cost.

Ethereal Threads of Nighttime

In the stillness of midnight's embrace,
Ethereal threads weave silk in space.
Stars embroider the darkened sky,
Stitching moments, the hours fly.

A tapestry spun in shadows deep,
Where secrets of night softly creep.
Moonlight glimmers on fragile dreams,
Whispers flow like gentle streams.

Woven softly in twilight's breath,
Life and dreams entwined in death.
Each heartbeat pulses with stories told,
In nighttime's fabric, the brave and bold.

Emerge from darkness, we find the light,
In ethereal threads, our futures bright.
Together we weave the night's embrace,
Through delicate strands, we find our place.

Radiant Heartbeats of Fantasy

Beneath a sky of vibrant hues,
Radiant heartbeats sing the muse.
Whirling colors, alive, they dance,
Inviting the dreamers into a trance.

Every pulse a story unfolds,
In realms where magic dares to hold.
With wings of hope, our spirits glide,
In the heart of fantasy, we take pride.

Echoes of laughter in the breeze,
Awakening dreams with joyful ease.
Through fields of wonder, we run free,
In radiant beats of melody.

Together we soar, hand in hand,
In this fantasy, forever we stand.
With every heartbeat, a spark ignites,
In radiant dreams, our souls take flight.

.

The Radiance of Reveries

In soft whispers of the night,
Dreams take flight, a silent sight.
Stars engage in timeless dance,
Guiding hearts in gentle trance.

From shadows deep, the light breaks free,
Painting worlds with vivid glee.
Every thought, a glowing spark,
Illuminates the journey's arc.

Awake, we chase the morning's glow,
Yet in dreams, the rivers flow.
Through the haze, our souls can reach,
The stories nature longs to teach.

In a realm where wishes soar,
Radiance awaits beyond the door.
Each reverie, a cherished gift,
In the silence, our spirits lift.

Luminous Journeys Beyond Sleep

In the twilight, shadows fade,
We embark, our dreams displayed.
Guided by the moon's embrace,
Wandering to a wondrous place.

With every star, our spirits rise,
Exploring realms beyond the skies.
Time dissolves in joyful play,
As night turns softly into day.

Echoes of the night unwind,
Whispers of the heart combined.
In twilight's grace, we find our song,
A tapestry where we belong.

Each journey pulls us from the shore,
To places known forevermore.
With every dream, our souls ignite,
Illuminating boundless night.

Aurora of the Imagination

As dawn ignites the hallowed sky,
Imagination begins to fly.
Colors dance in morning's light,
Unveiling visions, pure and bright.

With every thought, new worlds are born,
Ideas blossom, fears are shorn.
Within our hearts, we boldly tread,
Where visions guide and dreams are fed.

In this space, the magic swells,
Stories woven, time compels.
The canvas waits, a tale to weave,
In every heartbeat, we believe.

Auroras blaze, horizons stretch,
Each moment crafted, dreams etched.
In the light, we find our truth,
A symphony of joy and youth.

Shimmering Pathways to Wonder

Through forests deep and rivers wide,
Shimmering pathways, side by side.
Every step a dance of grace,
Leading us to a sacred space.

In the glimmer of the night,
Secrets whisper, pure delight.
Each pathway glows with hidden dreams,
Guiding hearts with silver beams.

Beneath the stars, we wander free,
Finding treasures yet to see.
With every twist, the journey calls,
Echoes of love that never falls.

To wonder's edge, we take the leap,
On shimmering roads that softly sweep.
In the light of possibilities,
We find our dreams, our destinies.

Serene Flickers

In quiet nights the stars ignite,
Soft glimmers dance in muted light.
A gentle breeze will weave and sway,
As dreams ascend on wings of play.

The moon reflects a silver stream,
Casting shadows on the gleam.
Whispers of the night hold tight,
In tranquil gardens, pure delight.

Each flicker speaks a silent tale,
Of hearts that dream and hopes that sail.
A moment stolen, still and clear,
Serene flickers draw us near.

With every twinkle, time does cease,
In this beauty, find your peace.
A canvas vast, a cosmic sea,
The night unveils its mystery.

Dancing with Daydreams

In fields of gold where wildflowers sway,
I lose myself, where thoughts can play.
The sun dips low, a brush of hue,
As daydreams dance, my spirit flew.

Clouds like whispers softly glide,
Carrying wishes, dreams abide.
Each gentle step, a glint of grace,
In this vast and open space.

Melodies of the heart arise,
As laughter twinkles in the skies.
I waltz through moments, light and free,
With daydreams as my company.

The world melts into shades of peace,
As all my worries find release.
In this soft glow, I am alive,
Dancing where my dreams survive.

Shadows that Shine

In twilight's grasp, where light meets dark,
Shadows gather, kindling a spark.
They dance with echoes from the past,
In fleeting moments, shadows cast.

A hidden grace within their form,
Emerging softly, breaking norm.
Each silhouette tells stories old,
In quiet whispers, tales unfold.

They shimmer softly, light to find,
In every corner, shadows bind.
Carving space where dreams align,
In the glow, these shadows shine.

They wrap the night in mystery,
A blend of dark and history.
Through every line, they sketch divine,
In the delicate art of shadow's design.

Whispers of the Luminous

Among the stars, a secret hum,
A call to hearts where dreams become.
In radiant blooms that softly glow,
The whispers rise, as soft winds blow.

The dawn ignites with colors bright,
Painting stories in morning light.
Each petal holds a tale to share,
In whispers, love fills the air.

With every breath, the world does sigh,
In luminescence, dreams will fly.
A tapestry of moments spun,
In every whisper, there's a sun.

So let the light fill up your soul,
And guide you gently, make you whole.
In every flicker, every gleam,
Find whispers of a timeless dream.

Echoes of Spirited Wanderings

Footfalls dance on ancient stones,
A melody of time's soft moans.
Through shadowed woods where whispers flow,
The tales of wanderers begin to grow.

Beneath the canopy of endless skies,
Hope flickers bright in the twilight lies.
With every breath, the spirits sing,
In harmony with the joy they bring.

Branches sway in the evening breeze,
Carrying secrets of the trees.
Echoes blend with the stars above,
In this realm of dreams and love.

Awakened hearts chase fleeting light,
Guided by the moon's soft sight.
Together they roam, forever entwined,
In the echoes of a world so kind.

Enchanted Pathways Through Slumber

Through veils of dream, the pathways weave,
With colors bright that never leave.
Treading softly on a misty ground,
Where hidden wonders can be found.

The stars align with a gentle glow,
Leading the way where mortals go.
In whispers sweet, the night reveals,
The magic wrapped in surreal feels.

Moonlit flowers bloom in grace,
Unfolding dreams in this sacred space.
The breeze carries tales of yore,
As sleep entices to explore.

Awakened spirits, bold and free,
Dance along this reverie.
In slumber's arms, the night takes flight,
Through enchanted pathways of pure light.

Whispers of Midnight

In the hush of night, secrets dwell,
Under the moon's enchanting spell.
Shadows play and softly glide,
Where dreams and hopes do often bide.

Stars twinkle in the velvet sky,
Casting wishes that never die.
With every sigh, a story born,
In whispered thoughts, we are reborn.

The world sleeps, yet hearts awake,
Embracing love, no fear to take.
Each gentle touch, a fleeting kiss,
In the magic of this midnight bliss.

Time stands still, the night unfolds,
A tapestry of dreams retold.
In the silence, the heart will find,
The whispers of midnight, sweet and kind.

Illuminated Wishes

Under the starlit, vast expanse,
Wishes dance in a cosmic trance.
Dreams wander through the endless night,
Chasing the glow of soft twilight.

Each flickering flame carries a prayer,
Floating high in the midnight air.
They whisper secrets to the sky,
As hopes and fears so gently fly.

In the stillness, the heart must dare,
To reach for magic, pure and rare.
Embers spark in the deepest mind,
Illuminated paths we seek to find.

The lanterns burn with promises true,
Guiding souls to start anew.
In every wish, a chance to be,
Illuminated in serenity.

Twilight's Embrace

The sun dips low, a soft goodbye,
Colors blend in the vastened sky.
Birds return to their cozy nests,
As night unfolds in dusky vests.

Whispers of stars begin to gleam,
Cool breezes carry a silent dream.
In shadows cast, secrets reside,
In twilight's glow, where hearts confide.

Night's curtain falls, the world is still,
Moonlight bathes the earth with thrill.
A gentle touch of evening's grace,
All nature sighs in twilight's embrace.

As dreams take flight on silver beams,
The night reveals its tender themes.
Embers of hope softly ignite,
In the stillness of the night.

Dream Chaser's Tale

A wanderer tall, with eyes so bright,
Chasing the stars through the veil of night.
With every step, a story unfolds,
In whispers of magic and tales of old.

Through valleys deep and mountains high,
He seeks the dawn, the limitless sky.
With passion fierce, he runs with grace,
The rhythm of life in every pace.

In dreams he flies, on wings of gold,
Grasping the magic the night has told.
Each wish a note in his melody,
A symphony of possibility.

As the morning breaks, the chase goes on,
In every heart, a new dawn's song.
For dreamers will chase what lies ahead,
In fields of wonder, where dreams are bred.

When Wishes Dance in Light

Under the moon's soft, silver glow,
Wishes are whispered, as breezes flow.
Stars weave stories in skies so bright,
As dreams take shape in the gentle night.

Fluttering sparks in the dark arise,
Casting their magic across the skies.
Hearts entwined in a luminous trance,
As hopes take flight in a cosmic dance.

With every flicker, a secret told,
Of dreams that shimmer like threads of gold.
In the silence, love's whispers ignite,
When wishes dance in the softest light.

So close your eyes, let your heart believe,
In realms of wonder, where dreams achieve.
For in this moment, anything's bright,
When wishes dance, when wishes take flight.

Beyond the Spectrum

A world unseen, where colors blend,
In shades of twilight that never end.
The spectrum calls, a melody sweet,
In every heartbeat, magic we meet.

Past the horizon where dreams are spun,
Infinite realms, where souls can run.
Each hue a whisper, each shade a song,
In the hands of time, we all belong.

Journeying through, our spirits soar,
In colors vivid, forevermore.
Beyond the spectrum, we find our way,
In the tapestry of night and day.

So let us wander where rainbows play,
In sacred realms where shadows sway.
For in this expanse, our hearts connect,
Beyond the spectrum, we find respect.

Cosmic Whispers of Tomorrow

In stars, the secrets softly gleam,
Woven threads of a distant dream.
Galaxies spin, a cosmic dance,
Whispered hopes in a starry trance.

Winds of time, they pull and sway,
Guiding lost souls on their way.
Each heartbeat echoes, faint yet clear,
Messages from futures near.

Nebulae bloom in colored light,
Painting visions in the night.
Infinity calls with a gentle sigh,
In the vastness, we learn to fly.

Embrace the whispers, soft and sweet,
In every starlit pulse, we meet.
Cosmic wonders above us soar,
A boundless realm awaits, explore.

Lanterns of the Mind's Eye

Flickering thoughts like lanterns glow,
Illuminating paths we know.
Shadows dance on the walls of time,
In the silence, reason chimes.

Each flicker holds a tale untold,
Dreams and wishes, brave and bold.
Through the darkness, visions find,
Light the corners of the mind.

Candlelight whispers of days gone by,
With every flame, a gentle sigh.
Hearts entwined in twilight's hue,
Awakening wonders, deep and true.

Together, we'll wander, hand in hand,
Navigating this dreamland.
Lanterns guiding us through the night,
Illuminating our shared flight.

Dreamscapes Drenched in Light

In dreamscapes bright, we glide and sway,
Colors meld in a vibrant ballet.
Waves of joy in soft embrace,
Lost in time, a tranquil space.

Floating gently on fields of air,
Thoughts like petals, light as prayer.
Every wish takes flight, it seems,
In the tapestry of our dreams.

Radiant visions, bold and bright,
A dance of shadows, pure delight.
With each heartbeat, freedom calls,
Embrace the spark when daylight falls.

Awake, yet lost in twilight's song,
In this realm, we feel we belong.
Drenched in light, our spirits soar,
In the dreamscapes, we explore.

Celestial Dreams Unfolding

Celestial dreams in twilight's glow,
Unfold like petals, soft and slow.
In the stillness, wonders bloom,
Whispers of the night consume.

Stars align in a cosmic rhyme,
Each heartbeat marks the hands of time.
Galactic journeys, we embark,
With passion igniting every spark.

Beneath the moon, destinies weave,
With every breath, we dare believe.
In the silence, love will guide,
Through the universe, side by side.

Embrace the wonders, wide and free,
In celestial realms, just you and me.
Unfolding dreams in the night's embrace,
Together we soar to a timeless place.

Glowing Shadows

In the whispers of the night, they sway,
Dancing softly, secrets at play.
Beneath the moon's tender glow,
Shadows emerge, weaving slow.

In the dim light, dreams take flight,
Carried away by the gentle night.
Flickers of memory, old and new,
Creating a tapestry of shadowed hue.

In corners where no one goes,
Lies the beauty that silence knows.
Embraced by darkness, they find their way,
Glowing softly until the break of day.

Together they linger, a fleeting art,
Echoes of life, where shadows start.
A world unseen, yet full of grace,
In glowing shadows, we find our place.

Illuminated Paths of Desire

Beneath the stars, our dreams unfold,
Illuminated paths, stories told.
With every step, we chase the light,
Desires that gleam, burning bright.

Winding roads, they beckon us near,
Guided by hopes, we feel no fear.
Each turn unveils a hidden gate,
To realms of passion we create.

In the glow of moonlit skies,
Whispers of longing softly rise.
Through paths unknown, we journey forth,
Chasing the flame that gives us worth.

Forever onward, we'll boldly tread,
With hearts ablaze and love widespread.
For in this quest, we find our song,
Illuminated paths where we belong.

Flickers of Hope

In the dimmest light, there lies a spark,
Flickers of hope dispelling the dark.
A breath of courage, a whisper of cheer,
Guiding us gently, drawing us near.

Through storms of doubt, we wade and fight,
Each flicker ignites, a promise of light.
Lifting our spirits, they rise and soar,
In the heart of despair, we find we want more.

Each moment we pause, our dreams rescue,
Woven together, stitched with the true.
Flickers of hope, tiny yet bold,
Carrying stories that need to be told.

As shadows retreat, and dawn draws near,
The flickers grow bright, dispelling all fear.
In unity's glow, they shine as one,
Flickers of hope, a new day begun.

The Radiance of Possibilities

In the dawn's embrace, futures gleam,
The radiance of possibilities, a dream.
With every heartbeat, potential ignites,
Chasing horizons, reaching new heights.

Through the veil of uncertainty, we dare,
To grasp the unknown and breathe the air.
Colors of triumph paint our skies,
In the canvas of life, hope never dies.

With every step, the world expands,
The radiance glowing in our hands.
Infinite paths await our tread,
In the journey of dreams, all fears shed.

Together we shine, a guiding light,
In the tapestry woven, love takes flight.
The radiance of possibilities, ever bright,
Inviting us forward, igniting the night.

Flickers of Tomorrow

In shadows deep where secrets dwell,
A spark ignites, a silent bell.
Whispers dance on twilight's breath,
Hope reborn, defying death.

Stars align, the night takes flight,
Casting dreams on paths of light.
With every flicker, futures gleam,
A tapestry woven from a dream.

Time slips softly, a fleeting tide,
Carving journeys where hearts collide.
In the hush of dawn's embrace,
We find the courage to embrace.

So let us chase what lies ahead,
With flickers bright, our spirits fed.
Together we'll forge a new dawn,
In the glow of a future born.

A Canvas of Light

Brush of dawn paints skies anew,
Colors swirl in morning dew.
A canvas stretched, the world awake,
Each stroke a promise we all make.

Golden hues in a lover's gaze,
Bright as sun through autumn's haze.
With every heartbeat, art unfolds,
A story whispered, life retold.

Stars reflect in a lover's eyes,
Mapping constellations in the skies.
Through night's embrace, we'll find our way,
Crafting dreams that softly sway.

In the silence, visions bloom,
Filling corners of the room.
A canvas glows with life in sight,
Framed in tenderness, a dance of light.

The Dreamcatcher's Lantern

In twilight's glow, hope takes its flight,
A lantern shines, chasing the night.
Dreams entwined in silken thread,
Caught in whispers of all that's said.

Stars ignite in a velvet sky,
To catch our dreams as they flutter by.
Each flicker, a wish, a guiding hand,
Crafting futures as we stand.

Beneath the moon's enchanting gleam,
We weave together a magic dream.
The lantern's glow, a tender guide,
Illuminates where hearts confide.

In every shadow, light shall gleam,
With every heartbeat, we chase the dream.
The dreamcatcher's lantern held up high,
Guiding lost souls, as time slips by.

Awakened Illumination

Amidst the dawn, the light appears,
Waking souls, dispelling fears.
Each ray a whisper, soft and sweet,
An invitation, pure and neat.

Emerging from the night's embrace,
Clarity found in time and space.
All burdens lift with morning's glow,
Awakened hearts begin to grow.

In this light, confusion wanes,
A brighter path through life's terrains.
Empowered voices rise and sing,
Harmony in everything.

With every breath, we find our way,
In brilliant hues, we greet the day.
Awakened with the sun so bright,
Together, we'll bask in shared light.

Whirlwind of Glow

In fields where fireflies dance at night,
A whirlwind of glow, pure and bright.
They twirl and spin in soft, warm air,
Whispers of magic, light everywhere.

With every flicker, dreams take flight,
Guiding the lost with gentle light.
Through shadowed paths, they lead the way,
A symphony of hope in night's ballet.

In hearts they spark a longing flame,
A promise whispered, never the same.
Together we chase, the stars and more,
In this whirlwind glow, we yearn to explore.

So let us dance 'neath the vast, deep sky,
Where fireflies flicker and spirits fly.
In the whirlwind of glow, we find our place,
A timeless moment, a warm embrace.

Shadows in the Daybreak

As night retreats, the shadows play,
In delicate lines, they weave the day.
Soft hues emerge from the curtain wide,
Where secrets linger, dreams abide.

The sun spills gold on waking earth,
A gentle glow, embracing worth.
While shadows stretch, they dance and sway,
In harmony with the breaking day.

Whispers of dawn, a silent song,
Guiding the world, where hearts belong.
In every shadow, a story told,
Of fleeting moments, both young and old.

Through valleys deep and mountains high,
Shadows linger, bidding goodbye.
As day unfolds, they fade away,
A fleeting dance in bright array.

Enveloping Radiance

In the hush of morning, a glow appears,
Enveloping all, calming fears.
It wraps the earth in soft embrace,
Illuminating dreams in a gentle space.

A tapestry woven with threads of light,
Radiance spills, banishing night.
With petals blooming, colors unfold,
A symphony painted in hues of gold.

Each ray that dances on the stream,
Whispers of hope, ignites the dream.
The world awakens, alive and bright,
In this enveloping, wondrous light.

So let us stand, hand in hand,
Beneath the radiance, vast and grand.
In moments shared, we find our song,
In the heart of light, where we belong.

An Odyssey through Light

Journey we take, through streams of light,
An odyssey bright, into the night.
Paths intertwined, where shadows lie,
A beacon of hope in the darkened sky.

We chase the dawn, with hearts so bold,
Finding warmth where dreams unfold.
In every gleam, a story starts,
Connecting souls with glowing parts.

Through forests deep and oceans wide,
The light our guide, where dreams reside.
In laughter shared and tears we shed,
An odyssey through light we tread.

Together we roam, hand in hand,
With every shimmer, our spirits stand.
In this vast journey, we dare to aspire,
An odyssey through light, forever inspired.

Whispers of Starlit Visions

In the quiet of the night, hearts awake,
Stars weave dreams, for our souls to take.
Whispers of the cosmos, soft and clear,
Guiding our desires, drawing us near.

Gentle breezes carry secrets untold,
Mysteries unfold, as the night grows bold.
Velvet skies draped in shimmering light,
Embracing our hopes in their cosmic flight.

Galaxies dance, a celestial waltz,
Igniting the spark of our inner pulse.
With every flicker, a story begins,
In this starlit realm, where magic spins.

Together we wander, hand in hand,
Through the tapestry woven by the grand.
In whispers and wishes, we find our way,
Under the watch of the night's array.

Dances in the Moonbeam Shadows

In the glow of the moon, shadows play,
Whirling and twirling, they dance and sway.
The night whispers softly, secrets abound,
In the luminescent glow, joy is found.

Footsteps of starlight on silken ground,
Echoes of laughter in movements unbound.
Twinkling stars join the jubilant spree,
As moonbeams weave magic with glee.

Each shadow a story, each glimmer a dream,
In the nocturnal ballet, we flow like a stream.
As the night wraps around, holding us tight,
We lose ourselves in the dance of the night.

With every soft sigh, a memory's spun,
In the moonbeam shadows, our hearts become one.
Together in rhythm, we sway and glide,
In the dance of forever, with love as our guide.

When Fantasies Take Flight

Upon the wings of dreams, we soar,
Fantasies unfurl, opening doors.
With every heartbeat, new worlds arise,
Painting the canvas of endless skies.

Imagination ignites like a spark,
Leading us through the boundless dark.
Each thought a feather, light and free,
Carving our path in the vast esprit.

Clouds of wonder cushion our fall,
Drifting through realms, we hear the call.
Adventure awaits in the whispers of night,
When dreams take wing and take to flight.

Together we chase the stars above,
In the playground of dreams, guided by love.
With open hearts, we embrace the light,
As fantasies twirl, ready for flight.

Illuminated Echoes of the Night

The night speaks softly, echoing dreams,
Illuminated visions flow like streams.
In shadows that dance, we find our place,
A tapestry woven, a sacred space.

Stars wink conspiratorially at our sighs,
In the hush of the night, the universe tries.
To unravel the secrets of hearts so bright,
Guiding us home by the flicker of light.

Whispers linger on the cool, crisp air,
In each illuminated moment, we dare.
To dive into depth, explore what we find,
In the echoes of night, our spirits unwind.

Together we journey, through dark and through glow,
In the realm of the night, forever we flow.
With a spark in our hearts, we'll dance and ignite,
In the illuminated echoes, we shine ever bright.

Twilight Serenade of Aspirations

In twilight's glow, dreams take flight,
Whispers of hope in the fading light.
Stars awaken, one by one,
Guiding the heart till the day is done.

A serenade of wishes breathe,
Floating softly on the evening's wreath.
Each note dances through the air,
Embracing the night with tender care.

Beneath the sky, ambitions soar,
Collecting shadows, longing for more.
The horizon blurs, future untold,
In this twilight, our dreams unfold.

Shadows Painted with Light

In corners where secrets reside,
Shadows play, they twist and glide.
Softly painted with hues of gold,
Stories of whispers quietly unfold.

The sun dips low, casting a spell,
Where light and dark weave tales to tell.
In moments of grace, they intertwine,
Creating a canvas, pure and divine.

Each shadow whispers, soft and low,
Of countless paths that we might go.
With every footstep, light will gleam,
In this dance of shadows, we find our dream.

Secrets Beneath the Silver Sky

Underneath the silver sky,
Lies a world where spirits fly.
Secrets linger in the breeze,
Whispered softly through the trees.

Moonlit paths invite the roam,
Guiding souls to find a home.
Stars above, like eyes so bright,
Guarding dreams through the night.

Hidden wonders come alive,
In the stillness, they will thrive.
Each glance up reveals the truth,
Of innocence, of lasting youth.

Glimmers of Enchantment

In the heart of a forest deep,
Glimmers of enchantment gently creep.
Fairy lights twinkle and gleam,
Turning the night into a dream.

With every step, magic unfolds,
Whispers of nature, secrets told.
In the hush of dusk's embrace,
A spell of stillness fills the space.

The air is thick with tales of old,
Of wishes granted and dreams bold.
Under the canopy, we roam free,
Chasing glimmers of what could be.

Glimmering Horizons

The sun dips low, a golden sphere,
Painting skies where dreams appear.
Whispers of hope in the gentle breeze,
Guiding hearts with subtle ease.

Mountains rise, their peaks aglow,
In twilight's breath, soft shadows flow.
Each star ignites, a distant spark,
Illuminating the tranquil dark.

Rivers weave through valleys wide,
Reflecting magic, where secrets bide.
Nature's palette, vibrant and grand,
Speaks of wonders across the land.

As night descends, the world finds peace,
In glimmering horizons, worries cease.
Embrace the charm of the endless skies,
Where every heart can learn to rise.

Enchanted Visions

In gardens lush where fairies play,
Whispers weave through light of day.
Petals dance on a gentle breeze,
Painting dreams amid the trees.

Moonlit paths of silver thread,
Lead to secrets, long since said.
Each shadow holds a tale untold,
In enchanted visions, brave and bold.

Lakes reflect the starry night,
Mirroring the world's delight.
Ripples chase the gleaming rays,
Capturing magic in timeless ways.

Here in realms where hopes take flight,
Every heart becomes alight.
In every moment, beauty sings,
Filling souls with wondrous things.

Radiant Reveries

Awake in dreams where colors bloom,
Radiant visions dispel the gloom.
A canvas painted by the dawn,
Where shadows fade and light is drawn.

Morning breaks with a gentle sigh,
As birds take wing and spirits fly.
Each note sung in the golden air,
Whispers love in the moment's care.

In fields of green, lost in the light,
Nature's embrace, a pure delight.
Every petal, a story spun,
In radiant reveries, we become one.

So let us dream and dance away,
In the warmth of every day.
With open hearts, we'll find our way,
In the beauty of what we say.

Luminous Pathways

Beneath the stars, our footsteps trace,
Luminous pathways, a gentle embrace.
Each step we take ignites the night,
Leading souls toward the light.

Whispers guide through ancient trees,
Carried softly on the breeze.
With every turn, a secret found,
In luminous pathways, love is crowned.

The moonlight dances on the stream,
In this realm, we find our dream.
Echoes of laughter, pure and bright,
Together we chase the fading light.

Hands held tight, we journey forth,
With hope and joy, we claim our worth.
In the glow of paths that intertwine,
Our spirits soar, forever shine.

Milton Keynes UK
Ingram Content Group UK Ltd.
UKHW021144271024
450226UK00007B/77

9 789916 906644